# Everyday
## Glimpses of God

Inspiring true stories of God's presence among us

Deacon Anthony C. Bonacci

**Everyday Glimpses of God**
Inspiring true stories of God's presence among us.
**Deacon Anthony C. Bonacci**

Copyright (c) 2023 Deacon Anthony C. Bonacci

All rights reserved. No part of this book may be reproduced in any form without permission from the author or publisher, except as permitted by U.S. copyright law.

Cover Artist: **Emma Lentz**

All rights reserved. No part of this book may be reproduced in any form without permission from the author or publisher, except as permitted by U.S. copyright law.

To request permission contact the publisher at randyjohnson@ilncenter.com

ISBN: 978-1-945423-52-9
Printed in the United States of America and other locations globely.

Published by the Five Stones Publishing and Randall E. Johnson
www.ilncenter.com

# Dedication

To my four children, Lynn, Tina, Maria, and Anthony; and to my eight grandchildren, Kelsey, Christopher, Emma, Andrew, Noah, Logan, Jonah, and Carmen.

May the Lord guide, guard, and protect you always.

# Acknowledgments

Thanks to my granddaughter, Emma Lentz, a Senior in Visual Communications Design at Kent State University, for creating and designing the covers for this book. Thanks also to the clergy, parishioners, friends, and family members who generously contributed their stories to this book.

# Contents

| | |
|---|---:|
| Dedication | 2 |
| Acknowledgments | 3 |
| Forward | 7 |
| Preface | 9 |
| Our Family's Little Angel | 11 |
| Miracle in Marysville | 15 |
| My Christmas Angel | 19 |
| Fingers in the Snow | 21 |
| Divine Intervention | 23 |
| Jake's Surgery | 25 |
| My New Bible | 27 |
| Angel at Broad and High | 29 |
| Papa's Faith and Trust | 31 |
| Raising Winners: Living and Listening to God's Plan | 33 |
| God Spoke to Me | 39 |
| My Angel Phyllis | 41 |
| God's Surprising Ways | 43 |
| Our Christmas Angel | 47 |
| The Relic | 51 |
| God Provides | 53 |
| In the Blink of an Eye...There was Hope | 57 |
| Waiting For Her Guardian Angel | 61 |
| Mass at Camp | 65 |
| September 12- A God-Incident? | 67 |
| My Daughter Survived | 69 |
| Grandpa's Baby Patrick | 71 |
| My Conversion | 73 |
| A Sudden Passing | 75 |
| My Guardian Angel in the Snow | 79 |
| Inspired by an Angel | 83 |
| "Hooking" Brought Me Closer to Him | 85 |
| About The Author | 87 |

# Forward

It is truly a gift to have eyes to see and ears to hear the big and small ways that God is working in our everyday lives. Some refer to these times as "God-incidences," "God moments," or "God winks." I believe it's important to acknowledge and share these real-life stories, as Deacon Tony does in this beautiful book. These stories lift us up and encourage and inspire us on our walk with God.

God is always working in our lives. We know this in our hearts, but it's so powerful to give testimony to this in real life. Often God's works seem hidden, but sometimes we are given the grace to see, hear and feel his work in a tangible and even visible way. It is hoped that these stories will bring others closer to God.

In referring to God, I'm referring to the Holy Trinity — Father, Son, and Holy Spirit. On occasion, we sense that Our Lady or a particular saint is interceding on our behalf.

Sometimes God's ways are surprising, even astonishing (such as the physical healings in some of these stories) and we simply need to get out of the way and let Him do His work. Other times, we are called to cooperate with him — maybe it's a little nudge to do this or that (or not do it!) and by his grace we feel compelled to comply.

Being faithful to a daily prayer life, reading scripture, and frequenting the Eucharist and the sacrament of Reconciliation can help us become more attuned to God's promptings and his movement in our lives.

In my life, as I commit to daily prayer and sacramental life, I've become more aware of God's work in my everyday activities. Several times a week I share with my husband a story about God intervening on my behalf.

I know that it's God working when in my heart I have a sense that God is active — that He made something happen, helped me work on an issue, or clarify a priority. Often, it's clear that it's God working when I look back in hindsight and see his handiwork. We won't know for sure this side of heaven, but that's when we are called to rely upon our faith.

I pray that this book and the everyday stories of God working in peoples' lives encourages you, blesses you, and strengthens you on your walk with God.

*Lori Crock*

*Founder of Holy and Healthy Catholic*

*Dublin, Ohio*

# Preface

My first book, *Faith, Family, and Formation*, sub-titled God's Plan Revealed, was a memoir, the story of my physical and spiritual journey over seven decades.

In my second book, *Reflections for Everyday Life*, I offered reflections based on homilies I had presented during my 25 years as a Catholic deacon. In it, I shared true stories or experiences that illustrated the theme of each homily.

In this volume, I present true stories from my life and the lives of family, friends, and parishioners that clearly reveal God's revelations to us, moments or experiences when God is present in a special way.

A few of the stories may be considered miracles. A miracle is defined as "a surprising and welcome event that is not explicable by natural or scientific laws and is therefore considered to be the work of a divine agency; a highly improbable or extraordinary event, development, or accomplishment that brings very welcome consequences.

As Christians, we are familiar with the various "epiphanies" (manifestations) of God in the Scriptures, including the miracles of Jesus and God the Father's announced approval of His Son.

The stories presented here are introduced with a comment that sets the scene or describes the type of revelation in the story that follows. Some are stories of miraculous healings; some are visitations of angels; some are clear manifestations of the presence of God as evident by an unexplainable event or avoidance of danger.

As I celebrate the twenty-sixth anniversary of my ordination, my hope and prayer is that the reader will be reminded of similar situations in his/her life, be inspired to recognize God's unique revelations to them, and be encouraged and motivated to accept God's will with heartfelt gratitude.

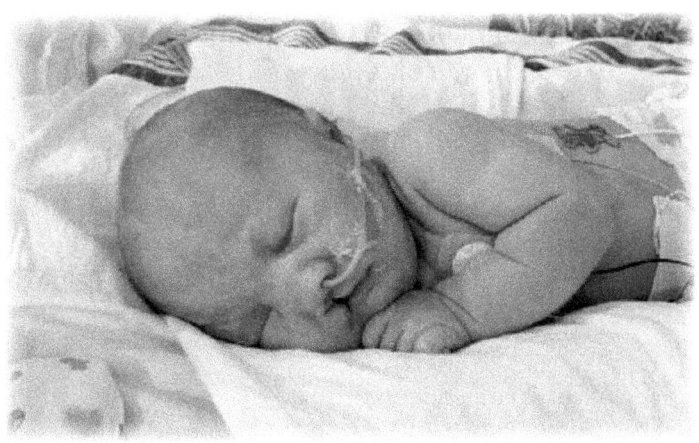

# Our Family's Little Angel

*This is the story of the miracle baby in our family. The following is an edited version of my brother's account of her birth and first two years, which was published in The Catholic Times of the Diocese of Columbus February 28, 2021.*

"Birthdays are for children!" My mom's words still ring in my ears. Perhaps what she meant is that as we age, we greet our birthdays with less enthusiasm. For me, I began to feel a bit uneasy once I became "Social Security eligible." At first, I was amused. Then, in what seemed like a blink of an eye, I found myself applying for Medicare! Thankfully, concerns over my advancing age ended in April of 2019.

During the early evening of my 65th birthday, our phone rang. It was my son-in-law. "You have a new granddaughter. Her name is Thea. Laura is fine but Thea has some medical issues." My wife and I raced to the hospital. As we arrived, Thea was being wheeled down the corridor to the Neo-Natal Intensive Care Unit with her dad at her side. She opened her beautiful blue eyes widely and greeted us. Minutes later, we visited our daughter who reminded me that Thea and I now shared a birthday. We were "birthday buddies". What a gift!

Several days later, Thea was transported to Nationwide Children's Hospital. After a series of tests, Thea was diagnosed with an extremely rare genetic disorder known as Trisomy 18. While Thea's condition was labelled "partial" Trisomy 18, her condition was no less serious. We learned that Thea was terminal. We were devastated. My mind raced to the beautifully decorated nursery that awaited her and the thought that she may never see it. We immediately made arrangements for Thea to be baptized that evening. My brother (Deacon Tony Bonacci) performed the Baptism in Thea's hospital room and our younger daughter Janine, a mother of three, proudly became Thea's Godmother.

Thea would spend the next three weeks at Children's Hospital. The medical care and emotional support Thea and her parents received from the doctors and nurses was exceptional, but unfortunately, Thea's diagnosis was confirmed. Thea's medical team assured her parents that Thea could remain in the hospital for as long as they would like. "Is there anything more you can do for Thea?", my daughter asked. "Unfortunately, not" was the response. "Then we want to take our daughter home" replied my daughter. Several days later, Thea was released and sent home on hospice care with her parents serving as her primary care givers. Possible future surgeries would be dependent upon Thea.

Surprisingly, months passed, and Thea was thriving at home in the comfort of her nursery and under the watchful eyes of her parents. Monitors checked her Oxygen saturation levels and heart rate. Portable and free-standing Oxygen tanks were utilized, allowing her parents to freely move her around the house. While her prognosis had not changed, it was apparent that Thea was enjoying her life at home. Although guarded, her doctors were amazed at her toughness and determination to survive.

In January 2020, Thea was readmitted to Children's for multiple surgeries. The goal was to improve her airway, insert a G Tube for feeding, repair her cleft lip and quite possibly, address a critical spinal cord issue. After nearly 5 hours of surgery, Thea emerged, but continued breathing difficulties required her to remain intubated for seven agonizing days. Thea would spend one full month at Children's Hospital during which time her lip healed magnificently, and slowly, her G tube became functional. During surgery, it was decided that her spinal cord issues would have to wait. Sadly, her breathing difficulties continued unabated.

Nevertheless, Thea once again defied the odds and returned home. Her mom and dad were educated on using her G tube, including reinserting it should it become disconnected from Thea's tiny abdomen. Unfortunately, Thea's breathing issues worsened, in the form of Apnea's. She would stop breathing, sometimes for several minutes, causing her parents to spring into action to revive her utilizing deep suctioning techniques and conventional CPR measures. Thea's medical team decided it was time for further intervention.

Several days before her 18th month birthday, Thea returned to Children's Hospital for an MRI of her brain and spine. Soon thereafter, she was scheduled for surgery on December 17, 2020. The purpose of this surgery was to further investigate her breathing difficulties, a hearing impairment, and if possible, to detach her tethered spinal cord. If uncorrected, her tethered spinal cord would eventually cause paralysis.

After nearly three hours of surgery, we were informed that Thea's spinal cord had been successfully "released", meaning that paralysis had been averted. In addition, we learned that the medical team had new ideas for addressing Thea's breathing and hearing difficulties. Thea was discharged from the hospital two days later. What a wonderful Christmas gift!

The devotion and emotional strength exhibited by our daughter and son in law during the past 20 months has been truly remarkable. They have inspired us with their unwavering optimism and unique confidence in Thea. Despite daily challenges, they are succeeding in furnishing Thea with the best life she can live each and every day. In return, Thea is providing her parents, family and all of her "prayer warriors" who have joined in her journey invaluable lessons in love, perseverance and faith.

As for my thoughts on future birthdays, I am looking forward to celebrating as many of them with my "birthday buddy" as the good Lord will allow.

Dennis J. Morrison
Hilliard, Ohio

Post Script: The following [edited] comments from Thea's doctor (Dr. Lisa Humphrey) were contained in an article by Doug Bean, Editor of The Catholic Times in that same issue:

"Among the many reasons I love my job is because I believe in miracles, love to bear witness to them, and my job is bountiful in both regards...I, like all people, have a hope for miracles...It is my job to look for them and honor their presence...to witness Thea's smile and its unabashed joy is a miracle...[for Thea to have] lived as long as she has is a miracle for me to behold...her parents' capacity to have followed their hearts so closely, advocated so well, and partnered so well with her medical team is the type of miracle I am honored to bear witness to and learn from."

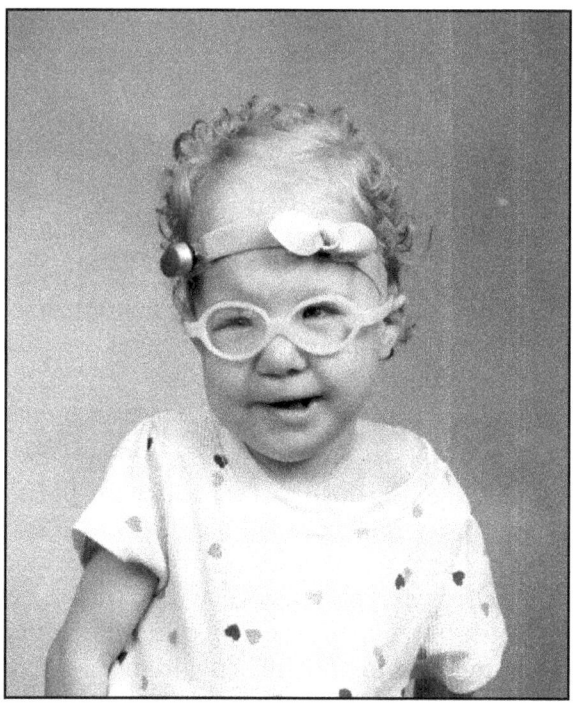

*Little Thea bravely lives on at four years old*

# Miracle in Marysville

*This is the (edited) true story of a Eucharistic miracle as reported by a Catholic priest in Marysville, Ohio in 2015.*

Many people believe in miracles. There are stories of healings, recoveries, and barriers that are broken that go well beyond the range of circumstance and "coincidence." People will share with you an incredible story that they can only explain as a miracle of the Divine, or they will share "little moments of grace" they attribute as God's little miracles.

As Catholics, we believe that ordinary bread and wine become the Body and Blood of Jesus Christ with the words of the consecration during Mass. Throughout our 2000-year history, there have been moments of revelation when God gives us a closer look into Eucharistic miracles. In the Eucharistic story that follows, it is left for the reader to decide whether this was an actual "miracle." Those who were privy to it have made up their own minds as to what they saw, witnessed, and experienced; for many, what did occur made us stronger in our Eucharistic faith.

The story begins in February of 2012. A very special and faith-filled couple had premature twins. Unfortunately, both babies only lived for minutes, but by the grace of God, both were baptized by local chaplains. With many tears and sorrow, we celebrated the Mass of Christian Burial and the girls were interred in a local cemetery near a young mother who had been interred there a few years before. That gave some comfort to the couple and to all of us who were in pain with them.

On Palm Sunday of 2012, as the mother was receiving the Eucharist, her infant son knocked the Host from her hand

and it landed on the floor. Flustered and panicked, she picked up the host and took it with her. Not sure what to do, she took the Host, which was in three pieces, to the cemetery and with a palm branch placed it at the grave of her infant babies. [Normally, a consecrated Host should be returned to the ground via a sacrarium (a sink that drains into the ground) or by direct burial into the ground.]

On the Sunday after Easter ("Divine Mercy Sunday"), the couple visited the babies' grave and noticed that the Host was still there, but that the white Host had significantly been altered and changed. Knowing that they had to share this discovery with me, they came to me and told me what they had seen. I went to the grave site with them, thinking that the Host had probably been "weathered" in some way. Anticipating that I would bury the Host there, we approached the grave and discovered that the Sacred white Host had what I would call red "veins" throughout its substance. These "veins" were bright red – blood red. In shock and awe, I carefully examined the Host. I could not draw any substantial conclusions other than this truly was the Body of Christ, in a very unique and miraculous way!

After burying the Host there, we returned home, but emotionally distraught, I knew I had to confer with the bishop. He suggested that I should reclaim the Host from the ground and dissolve it in the church's sacrarium. I returned to the cemetery with several witnesses. I will never forget the look on everyone's faces when I retrieved the Host. Most were moved to tears upon seeing it. After a few minutes, we carefully and reverently brought it to the church and dissolved it under running water in the sacrarium. All of us were awestruck and speechless. I commented how it felt like "flesh" disintegrating between my fingers.

Not much was said between us after that day; we all needed time to process what we had witnessed; time to figure out what God was saying to the couple and to all of us. A few months later, on the "due date" of the babies, I met with them, and we documented the series of events in some detail.

Three years later, we met again, and the couple shared that every day that God gives them is precious. They said, "God will take care of you; He's here, He's real!" and "Don't question your faith; we want people to know; we want people to know Him!"

This couple, now with four children, continue to raise their family in prayer and faith and have a deep love for the Eucharist. I believe the events that occurred have reinforced their beliefs to carry them through their pilgrimage until that glorious day when they can hold their twin girls in heaven.

*Father David Poliafico*

*Columbus, Ohio*

# My Christmas Angel

*This is a story of how one of God's messengers was there to minister to me.*

Just before Christmas of 1998, I experienced the presence of a "Christmas angel." I had been admitted to O.S.U. hospital through the E.R. after fainting at home. When I arrived at my room, my young roommate gave a little smile as I introduced myself, but was otherwise very private. I asked his name, and he said simply, "John." When I asked him what brought him into the hospital, he said, "diabetes." When I inquired about family, he said, "Oh, they're here somewhere..." (I found out later that he had not had even one visitor even though he had been there three and one half weeks). When I asked what kind of work he did, he chuckled and said simply, "construction."

I couldn't help overhearing his conversation with a social worker when she said she was "getting him some medications and diabetic supplies to last him for a while, and some information on organizations for the homeless." She said he would be discharged the next day. All day the next day, he kept saying his "friend" would come by and pick him up, but he seemed to be stalling. (It was a cold, snowy day outside.) While he was in the bathroom, I asked the nurse, "Does he have a place to go; does he have any money?" She said she didn't know, but her sympathetic look said she did know.

As it got dark, I heard him call a cab, and I decided to offer him some cash when he left. I was on the phone with my sister when all of a sudden, he drew back the drapes and bolted out the door, wearing only a tee shirt and jeans, and with no suitcase. I called out to him, "Hey, John," as I fumbled for my wallet; I thought I would slip him at least a twenty-dollar bill. That's when the strangest thing happened. John kept right on going, giving me a little smile over his shoulder, and waving at me with the back of his hand. I heard a quick, "Bye," and he was gone.

When I told my sister what had just happened, she said, "Maybe John was your Christmas angel, and maybe his work was done." Maybe he was, because the next morning the doctor said, "You know that blood draw we did last night? Well, your lab values have started to turn around; you've turned the corner!" So was it a "co-incidence?" Or was John on a mission?

*Deacon Anthony C. Bonacci*

*Plain City, Ohio*

# Fingers in the Snow

*This is truly a story of Divine intervention, as told by one of our parishioners.*

In the 1990's, we were living in our country home and driving to and from our jobs in Columbus each day. There were several brutal winters in those years, and everyone dreaded the country roads. However, I usually left home early to avoid traffic on the Interstate and a friend had told me how pretty the drive was on a particular country road.

One morning in early December, it was "precipitating" a mixture of rain, snow and slushy ice - a particularly nasty day. I was driving along in my nice warm car, being very careful and proceeding slowly. As I drove down the road, the temperature dropped, and the mix became very heavy snow. As I neared a mobile home park, my windshield wipers began to sputter. Then they quit altogether and froze up solid. I turned into the park and called my husband. I was beginning to realize that I would probably not make it to my office. My husband told me to stay in the car, keep the heater on, and that he would be there soon.

As I sat waiting for my husband, I was looking straight ahead at the group of mobile homes being covered with heavy snow. While watching the beautiful white stuff fall, I noticed a big fluff of snow suddenly pop UP from the ground. It was right at the edge of a home, a few feet from the entrance door. My first thought was a cat, playing or seeking shelter. Then I saw what looked like fingers! I continued to watch, not sure what I was seeing. The next thing I saw was a pale blue sleeve, on what I thought was a nightgown or a robe. I was approximately thirty feet away, and since I was wearing boots, I got out to investigate. I hurried, as I knew my husband would not be happy that I was NOT in my warm car with the motor running.

I fought my way through the snow and wind to the side of the home and bent down. I brushed some snow away, and found an elderly lady, buried in snow and partially hid by a trashcan. She was barely awake, confused and hardly able to move. She was tiny, so I was able to get under her arms and get her up. She was coming around a bit more and was able to lean on me as I half dragged her to her steps. Somehow, we got inside. I got a chair under her, and grabbed an afghan off her couch and wrapped her in it. I rubbed her hands, and she began to warm up. I started to call 911, but she asked me to call her daughter who lived nearby and could come right over. They insisted she would be ok. She drank hot tea, and explained that she had gone out, "only for a second" to get her newspaper. She had fallen and could not get up. The snow had quickly covered her.

When my husband got there, I told him about the incident and we cried with relief! I shudder to think what might have happened if I had not been forced to turn into that mobile home park.

We stopped back at the home in the Spring and were told that the lady had moved. We never even knew her name, but I could pick out her hand from the memory of it reaching through that snow, toward Heaven for help.

We can only pray that we do the right thing when God directs us to reach out to those who need our help.

*Gloria Butler*

*Plain City, Ohio*

# Divine Intervention

*This is the story of a healing in church; the touch of several faith-filled parishioners.*

One Sunday at Mass, I suddenly felt physically ill. The morning was cold, so I kept my jacket on while sitting. I could feel a cool breeze every time the entry door opened. After the gospel was read, the priest continued with the homily. My wife Donna was sitting beside me and taking notes as usual.

I then felt very warm and took off my jacket, feeling sweat on my face. I said to myself. "Check your blood sugar meter." I did, and it was 130, which was satisfactory. What was going on? My slacks were damp. my sweater was damp and I'm sure my shirt was wet also. I motioned to Donna that something was wrong, and she nodded, understanding my problem. She whispered, "Just sit there, and after Mass I'll get the car."

When the church emptied, several of my friends noticed me sitting quietly. My friend Marge, an RN, was next to me. She took my pulse and said it was a little low. She handed me a bottle of water and I drank it. The deacon approached me from behind and said, "a lady would like to pray for you; she is trained." She asked about eight people around me to lay their hands on me. I closed my eyes as I typically do when praying. She started praying in a soft tone in what I will call "deep prayer". Her voice sounded like it was close to my head.

After just a few moments I started to feel a coolness on my face, a comfortable feeling I had never felt before. Her voice was very comforting. I opened my eyes as she continued to pray and I could see on the faces of my friends that they were very concerned. Later, my wife Donna said my face went from pale to bright pink.

As this "stranger" continued with her prayers, a tear started to roll down my left cheek. The deacon said it was "a love tear." As her praying stopped some of my friends were attempting to get me to smile with some jokes. I did, but kept wondering, "What just happened? Who was this lady?"

Donna went to get the car and my friends stayed close beside me. I kept saying to myself, "I am so blessed." When we got home, I removed my wet clothing. I was tired and rested most of the day. On my next visit, my cardiologist said all was well and there were no changes since my last testing.

So was this "Divine Intervention?" It's not for me to say, but to this day, I have no idea what happened that morning.

*Ed Olenhouse*

*Hilliard, Ohio*

# Jake's Surgery

*This is the inspiring story of my Lutheran friend's strong faith in God's presence, first published in the Catholic Times of the Diocese of Columbus in February, 1992.*

On October 8, 1987, Albert "Jake" Leshy came up to me with a warm, gentle smile and said, "Hi, I'm Jake Leshy." I had just walked into the "Yellow Gym" in Larkins Hall at The Ohio State University to begin a Cardiac Rehab Program. Over some twenty years, we became best friends. We not only exercised together; we shared many visits, many blueberry pancakes at Bob Evans ("with extra blueberries"), and we shared our children's weddings, First Communions, Confirmations, holidays, anniversaries, birthdays... so many wonderful times...

In the Winter of 1992, I visited my Cardiac-Rehab friend Jake, who was then recovering from extensive urological surgery. Jake shared a personal and inspiring story about the days surrounding his ordeal...

About ten days before the surgery, he told his surgeon he would light two candles in the local Catholic Church, one for himself and one for the surgeon.

The day before the surgery, he was very anxious and concerned as he left his law office, so he decided to walk over to St. Joseph Cathedral to pray and light the candles for a safe and successful surgery. Jake warmly remembered that he had prayed and lit candles there on other occasions, especially in times of stress and concern.

As he waited for the office elevator in the very same spot he had stood every day for forty years, out of the corner of his eye he saw a sparkle of light from a nearby window. After waiting for the elevator a few more minutes, he again was drawn to the light. He turned toward the window, and the sparkle seemed to be persistent and attractive. As he walked to the window which looked down on the busy street, the sparkle seemed to grow into a larger soft glow.

Jake looked straight at the glow, which he now discovered was coming from something on the windowsill. He reached down and picked up a small pewter cross. Jake went to the cathedral to pray and light the candles as he had intended, reflecting on the meaning of finding the cross. In forty years, he had never seen anything on that windowsill. Yet, on that day and at this time, it appeared. Surely, it said to him, "I am with you."

The next day, as he went through the admission process, the admitting hostess said, "I see where Dr. Best is going to be your anesthesiologist." Jake questioned the name again and realized that the doctor named was a former neighbor many years before! He had apparently seen Jake's name on the surgery schedule and chose to be Jake's anesthesiologist for the surgery. Jake was again reassured of God's presence.

Throughout the entire five hours of surgery, the doctor sat by Jake

and was able to talk with him, as the anesthesia was the spinal type which allowed Jake to be awake. Jake also reminded the surgeon that he had indeed lit two candles, one for himself and one for the surgeon.

The surgery was a wonderful success. Jake's loving wife put the cross on a chain, and Jake wore it as a continuing reminder of God's presence for the rest of his life. My dear Lutheran friend passed peacefully with his wife and myself at his side in August of 2012.

*Deacon Anthony C. Bonacci*

*Plain City, Ohio*

# My New Bible

*This is a personal account of the "loss" and subsequent "find" of a lady's bible.*

Sitting at the nurse's station one ordinary day, I was approached by our Medical Director, a very intelligent and well versed physician who could discuss just about any subject. On this day, the subject drifted to the Bible. He politely asked me several difficult questions challenging the accuracy and truths of the Bible, pulling up several passages on his cell phone Bible to support his point, and leaving me speechless.

I left that day determined to look up some of his assertions and dispute them. At home I looked for one of our several Bibles, but couldn't find one. I asked my son if he knew where any of our Bibles might be, but every place where they typically sat for many years was vacant.

For weeks, we searched for one of our Bibles with no success. After several months, on an exceptionally hot Summer day, I was stopped by a slow moving train on my way to work. The line of cars was long and several turned around to go back the way they came. I patiently waited with my air conditioner running, but after a lengthy wait, decided to turn my car off. I put the windows down and settled in for a long, hot boring wait. I glanced over to my purse sitting on the passenger's seat, with the window down, and realized this might be dangerous. Anyone could reach in and steal my purse. No sooner had that thought left my mind, when I saw a large figure approach the passenger's side of my vehicle! I gasped as the arm of a man reached through the open window.

A deep male voice said "Jesus loves you" as he dropped a Bible onto the seat. I looked up to see a nondescript man in his late 20's wearing a grey t-shirt and baggy jeans walking away. My initial thought was this was an evangelist dropping off Bibles to every vehicle. But he had no other Bibles in his hands. I quickly paged through the Bible for a card or pamphlet promoting a religion or group but found none. This King James Bible is fondly known as my "car Bible" and has not left my vehicle since that extraordinary day. Shortly after this Bible arrived, we found all our "home" Bibles.

*Sandra Hilbert*

*Plain City, Ohio*

# Angel at Broad and High

*This is a story of an angel at a busy intersection.*

I grew up in a devout Catholic family in Columbus, Ohio where we belonged to St. James the Less parish. There we learned about God, the Angels and Saints, and the Holy Family. I attended the first, second and third grades there, until my parents could no longer afford the tuition. I remember being so excited to make my First Communion in the second grade. I loved learning about Jesus and what He did for us. When I was young and the kids would make fun of me, I would always tell them "God lives in your heart."

One of the things I also fondly remember is learning about Guardian Angels. I was always told I had one. I never in a million years thought I would ever meet mine face to face!

In my early 20s, I was working my first legal secretarial job in downtown Columbus, where I used to enjoy going for a walk after lunch, usually down Broad Street to the Scioto River. I loved just gazing over the river and enjoying nature. It made me forget all the hustle and bustle of downtown traffic.

One day on my lunch break, I decided to walk down toward the river to get some fresh air. I was having a hard day and had been feeling melancholy and a little overwhelmed. At the corner of Broad Street and High, one of the busiest intersections in downtown Columbus, the Walk sign flashed, and I started walking out into the intersection. Apparently, I did not hear or see a car speeding down High Street. A gentleman came out of nowhere, and suddenly pulled me back to the curb. He apologized for grabbing me but said he didn't want me to get hit. It scared me because I didn't see or hear the car until he pulled me back. Meanwhile, the car sped through the pedestrian crossing. I thanked him profusely as my heart pounded hard and my body shook. He walked with me across the street, told me to "take care," and walked the other way down High Street. I was almost in tears.

The next day, I was riding on a COTA bus on my way home from work when I saw that same man get on the bus and sit directly in front of me. He turned around and I noticed his kind eyes and true concern. He asked how I was and smiled at me. It was then that I noticed he had a name tag on. The name on it was "John Eric," the very same name as one of my older brothers who had died shortly after he was born. I was in shock and was sure he was my Guardian Angel. I never saw this man again.

Do I remember what he looked like? Yes, he was an average looking guy with light brown hair, very kind eyes, and a warm smile. I still think of him and ask God to send my Guardian Angel to protect me every time I walk to or from my car before or after work. I cannot wait to see him again and thank him again!

*Paula Dubosh*

*Plain City, Ohio*

# Papa's Faith and Trust

*This article is an edited version of my sister Marge's article published in the Catholic Times of the Diocese of Columbus in February, 2002.*

My father "Teddy," was a big man, kind and gentle, always the good father and husband. As he used to say, he "went through many trials and tribulations" in his life. But he always said that it was his "faith and trust in the good Lord" that got him through the rough spots.

After courageously supporting my mother through a five year battle with cancer, Dad accepted her death in 1977 as God's will without any bitterness. At the time, he said to my younger brother, "We will never get over this, but we will learn to live with it."

He tried living alone for a while, but after his several bouts with depression, my siblings and I decided that he needed to live with family for his own physical and mental health. We devised a plan whereby he "rotated" to live in each of our five homes every few months. That went on for over ten years, with Dad accepting and enjoying living with his children and grandchildren. He knew all our neighbors and took walks every day through our neighborhoods.

An avid reader, he would go through the daily newspaper "backwards and forwards," as he would say. Sometimes, reacting to the negative news of the day, he would say, "The whole world's gone mad!" Other times he would say, "Most of what you worry about doesn't happen." We still laugh when we remember his famous line when he would spot a dessert, saying, "That pie (cake, cookie, etc.) is winking at me."

In 1994, while living with me, he suffered a serious illness that involved a long recuperation. From the very beginning, though, I knew that Jesus was with him. It started the day we left the hospital, when I noticed that an African violet on my windowsill that had never bloomed suddenly displayed three beautiful purple flowers. Was it just a coincidence that I had placed a picture of the smiling Jesus above the plant in the window frame? I told Papa, "See Papa, that's a sign of hope." He agreed with some hesitation in his voice.

After the hospitalization he was a bit depressed and discouraged because he needed private-duty nursing in our home. The first nurse who came was named "Faith." Once again, I said, "Jesus is watching over you, Papa." Soon after, I received the weekly schedule of the nurses who would be caring for him each day. The second nurse's name was "Teddy" (Papa's nickname). I was overwhelmed with a sense of God's presence as the weekly schedule read: "Faith-Teddy-Faith-Teddy-Faith-Teddy-Teddy."

Dad passed on peacefully at the age of 92 in 2004, having led a long and distinguished life. Because of his own short education, he always stressed the importance of education to his children and grandchildren. At the time of his passing, he had eleven grandchildren and nine great-grandchildren. His bedtime ritual included the words, "Good night, good luck, and God bless."

*Margaret Morrison Armillotti*

*Orchard Park, New York*

# Raising Winners: Living and Listening to God's Plan

*This is the inspiring and heart-warming story of a mother who discovered and shares her true "mission" in life.*

It started with a perfectly kind woman at the grocery store. "Wow, they are both yours, and you are having another! You must have always wanted a lot of kids?" She really would have been shocked if I told her my oldest was in preschool, giving me a grand total of 4 under 4. I slowly turned my giant pregnant self towards her, and responded with my usual, "Yep, all mine! It's crazy but I love it." To answer her question, I added, "Oh, yes I have always wanted a bunch!" So how did I get from there to crying on my bedroom floor throwing a tantrum which could only be rivaled by my 2-year-old? Well, it could be because I lied.

After our conversation, I quickly gathered my 1-year-old and 2-year-old into the van, headed for the nearest Starbucks, then headed to pick up my oldest, 4-year-old Leo, at preschool. As I sat in the parking lot, I began contemplating my grocery store experience. The kind woman at the cash register was not the first to comment on my family size. I heard it about 1000 times a day from well-meaning strangers. It never bothered me, but this time the question was different. Usually, it is just some snarky comment such as "you know how that happens, right?' But this question caught my attention; did I always want a lot of kids? To get down to it, the real answer is no.

I never really wanted a houseful of kids. As a young girl, I never even thought about babies. Sure, I would babysit for the occasional adorable neighbor baby and cuddle my nieces and nephews, but I was never going to go out of my way to spend time with baby/toddler. I didn't have anything against babies, they just weren't on my radar. I was much more interested in soccer, friends, travel, and being involved in the Church. I enjoyed sharing my faith with others and I wanted to live a life that involved helping others, serving Christ, and having fun. Babies didn't seem to fit into that picture.

I began to ponder what was I planning on doing after those college years before I blinked and somehow was married with a houseful of bouncing babies. The answer was easy. I wanted to enter religious life and be a missionary. Not a standard teenage girl's dream, but it was mine. Knowing it was a big countercultural move, I kept it to myself. I was going to go to college to acquire a degree in education or theology. I would make friends, date, experience life, join a religious order, then move to Africa and work in the missions.

I was going to travel, meet interesting people, help the needy, experience new cultures, and all the while spread the Gospel of Jesus Christ! I was going to live out God's plan. Devote my life to the Church, save souls, feed the poor. Just call me St. Emily! I was going to be the best Catholic you ever met. And it would be an amazing, adventurous life. And the thought began to consume me.

My life was anything but adventurous. Void of anything remotely adventurous, it was full of diapers, snacks, sippy cups, Storytime, crafts, tantrums, ABC's, breastfeeding, never sleeping (really never), and the hope that one day I will have time to brush my hair and my teeth in the same day. The most exciting thing I had was seeing if my husband and I could survive attending Mass with all the kids and everyone still making it out alive.

I continued. I prayed. I prayed the same prayer that I have muttered most of my life, "God, let me do what you want me to do. Speak loudly so I can hear you". I asked God to help me stay optimistic, see my blessings whatever they may be... and I carried on. After all, I loved my life in many ways. My husband is wonderful (and handsome to boot!), my kids are my joy, and I can't imagine going a day without snuggling these little ones. My unending, unconditional love of these little babies/toddlers is pretty strong evidence in God's grace. And through that grace, I even had a newfound love for everyone else's babies too. When out, whether at church, a party, even the grocery store I will now be one of those crazy old ladies that asks to hold your baby, because I just can't resist (you have been warned!).

But then a few days later, my sister called. "I am going to Africa!" She exclaimed. She told me all about how she was blessed with the chance to do a mission trip for two weeks. We chatted about the excitement of the opportunity, how mom and dad would be so worried... I promised to donate to the charity to help fund her trip. I hung up the phone, sat in my messy, tiny, loud, house and cried.

So, that is how I got here. Weeks of thinking about "what if" and my sister was now going to experience (in a small way), my dream, my adventure. I lamented how I can't even find a day to volunteer at the local Run the Race Center, let alone travel across the world sharing the love of Christ. How God must be so disappointed in me. How could I have messed this up? How could God let me give up on my dreams? It was not as if they were overly ambitious or selfish. I wasn't aiming to be the CEO of Google. I just wanted to live a life of service that pointed towards God and maybe have some amazing experiences along the way. I thought maybe too many years of mistakes, and one too many sins had blinded my heart and my ambitions, and I had missed my chance and didn't listen to God's call. I suppose I became distracted by the fun of being a 20-year-old girl and the charm of a tall, funny, Catholic boy. And stumbled to where I am now. I knew God was still faithful and had blessed me with this family, but my heart longed to know what could have been. The feeling that maybe I was doing something wrong and was not serving God enough lingered. I felt like I had disappointed him. In my whiny fit, I assumed either I messed up or God didn't know what he was doing. This was no life dedicated to improving our world. This was every day, ordinary Mom. I missed my chance to do something amazing and I would have to watch everyone else's adventures from home with a toddler on my leg and a baby in my arms.

Ace knocked on the door sweetly asking to read a book. I quickly dried my tears and said a little prayer that went something like this. "I know I am overreacting, but I am allowed to have my moment, right? All I wanted to do was something special, and all I feel is stuck. Please, show me your plan Lord, and I promise I will follow it." I got up, read Little Blue Truck, and started to make dinner.

As the family gathered around the table I was still in a sober mood. I put the plates down, got everybody drinks, sat down, and started to eat - until I was interrupted by Leo. "Mom, you forgot to pray!" and I watched as my four-year-old led his little brothers (even the one-year-old holding his hands and mumbling along) perfectly saying their prayer.

Then it hit me. I was wrong. I was already a missionary and I didn't need to take a step out of Ohio to do it! The calling to care for and teach these adorable boys was just as honorable as traveling around the world teaching orphans. It was beyond a mission, it was my true vocation! God even blessed me with the man of my dreams to accompany me on this crazy journey. And together we get the privilege of serving God in our community and teaching our children to do the same. God knew my heart. My intentions were misplaced. My dreams were based on pride. On my mission. On my success. That is not what God wants from us. God calls us to totally abandon ourselves. We are reminded of this in Galatians; "I am crucified with Christ: nevertheless, I live; yet not I, but Christ lives in me: and the life which I now live in the flesh I live by the faith of the Son of God, who loved me, and gave himself for me."(Galatians 2:20)

I can only imagine what a selfish person I would have been without my children. I know a lot of people who say they don't need kids to know true love, or how to serve. Well, good for them. I do. I was a jerk, and I didn't even know it. God knew I needed a kick in the pants (or five kids kicks) to help me get over myself. A missionary focused on her accomplishments was not a missionary at all. So, he humbled me, to better me. To refine me. You know how Christmas day is way better as a parent, watching your kids' joy and excitement? I imagine that is true in the rest of life as well. So, for now, my adventures will consist of trips to the ER (they happen too often) and Friday night dance parties in our PJs. But I am more than okay with that. The mission of being a Catholic mother is not for the weak of heart. In fact, it is a challenge full of sacrifice, more than I ever could have imagined as a twenty-something college student. Let's talk more on how to live out the mission another day...

I recently bought a sign at Hobby Lobby: it says, 'You are our greatest adventure". And as I sit here with my (now 8) little souls, my heart couldn't be more content. I am full of joy and peace, the kind that only comes from knowing you are following God's call. I am grateful to have had the chance for God to remind me of this. I think I was able to hear his voice and follow his plan, even when I couldn't recognize it because there are two things I have never given up on: praying and attending Mass. I am not perfect, and I have done my share of sinning, but even in my darkest times I did not give up on prayer, Confession and Mass.

So, to you I say, "Keep your soul focused in prayer (Matthew 7:7), obey his commandments (John 14:15), and receive his grace in the Sacraments (John 6:35-71)." If we do these things, we will be certain to follow His plan, even when we feel like we can't read the blueprint. If things don't seem "perfect," they will be perfect in His time.

I love the verse in Jeremiah (it's one of our Family Bible Verses the boys have memorized): God promises, "For I know the plans I have for you. A plan for you to prosper, to give you hope and a future". (Jeremiah 29:20) I don't know exactly what my future will be, but I know I never could have imagined life being this beautiful. Even my best plan was completely lacking in love, joy, and sacrifice compared to what I have now. I know that the best part of my future will be standing side by side with my husband watching our children live their own dreams. And who knows. Maybe, just maybe, one of them will grow up to be a missionary.

So, to my children I say, "Always keep hope, be confident in your future, never give up on your dreams, and always keep God's plan close to your heart. You never know what adventures he has for you."

*Mrs. Emily Winner*

*Plain City, Ohio*

# God Spoke to Me

*This is a short and personal witness by a man whose life was changed by two sermons he heard during Lent.*

When I was in my 40's, I realized I had developed a drinking problem. My preferred drink was a vodka martini. I didn't drink every day, but once I started, it seemed I could not stop until I had emptied the bottle. Simply stated, I had become an alcoholic.

I started praying every day, "God, please don't let me let me drink today." But the pattern didn't really change. I didn't drink every day, but on days when I did, I could not stop with just one.

As we were approaching Lent one year, my pastor preached a sermon encouraging us to "give up" something for Lent that was very important to us. I saw an opportunity and thought, "Maybe I can give up drinking for 40 days."

Halfway through Lent, the pastor preached another sermon in which he said that whatever we gave up for Lent might be something we should give up for life. My first thought was, "Thanks a lot!" But then I thought, "Well, if I can give it up for 40 days, maybe I can give it up for 40 weeks. And if I can give it up for 40 weeks ..."

I am blessed to say I have not consumed a drop of alcohol for 34 years now . . . and counting.

I have always felt that the sermons/homilies I heard on those two days were meant specifically for me. A few years ago, I had the opportunity to tell the pastor what his words meant to me. When I thanked him for telling me exactly what I needed to hear, he said, "That wasn't me talking to you. That was God talking to you through me." As I look back on it, I am pretty sure that is exactly what happened, and I thank God every day.

*Dick Ogden*

*Plain City, Ohio*

# My Angel Phyllis

*This is a moving "Angel Story" that tells of a man's faith in God's messengers, His angels.*

I grew up in a family of four, three boys and a girl. My sister Phyllis and I were the middle children, and we were very close. She was four years older, and I looked up to her, often asking her for advice. Unfortunately, she died in September of 1996.

My father had always been an auto racing fan and would occasionally take my younger brother and I to the local racetrack in Toledo, Ohio. His dream was to attend the "granddaddy" of them all, the Indianapolis 500, which is always scheduled for Memorial Day weekend. We would watch the race on TV every year and wished we were there. Unfortunately, my father passed away in 1988 and never got to experience the live race.

In May of 1997, I was given four tickets and an opportunity to attend the Indianapolis 500. My wife decided to let our three children go with me. At the time, we lived in Springboro OH, a city south of Dayton, approximately one hundred and fifty miles from Indianapolis. The race is always planned for Sunday with Monday as a backup day if unable to race. Our only concern was the weather. The forecasters had predicted a window of opportunity to run the 2.5-hour race before anticipated storms, so we decided to go.

When we arrived, we visited the race museum, snacked, and proceeded to our seats. We enjoyed the activities prior to the race: the stealth bomber flyover, a parade of celebrities riding in convertibles, Jim Nabors singing "Back home in Indiana," the national anthem, and the traditional "Ladies and gentlemen, start your engines!" The cars started and we could hear the deafening roar of the engines and the cheering crowd.

The cars were on the second warm-up lap when it started to rain very hard. Since the cars cannot run on wet pavement the race was halted. We sat there for an hour or more in the pouring rain. Luckily, we were prepared with raincoats and umbrellas. After the rain ended, trucks outfitted with jet engines were used to dry the 2.5 mile track, which takes three hours. They were about ready to restart the race when it started to rain again. Since the race couldn't be completed before darkness, the race was called for the day and re-scheduled for the same time on Monday.

On Monday morning, we went through the same routine but the weather was a carbon copy of the day before. After we sat through more rain and attempts to dry the track, the race was postponed again and we departed for home. We were tired from getting up early and experiencing two long disappointing days. A short time later on the Interstate, all three children fell asleep. As I was driving toward home, I also felt tired, and then, the unimaginable happened – I fell asleep at the wheel!

I have no idea how long I slept, but I was suddenly startled awake by a loud voice saying "**Gregory, WAKE UP.**" My eyes opened to find myself driving in the passing lane, perfectly centered, and adequately spaced from the car in front of me. My heart was beating so hard I thought it would jump out of my chest. I am certain that the voice I heard belonged to my sister Phyllis, who always called me by my full first name ("Gregory") rather than "Greg." Clearly, a tragedy was averted that day. On that day, at that hour, my sister Phyllis, a beautiful, loving person and Godmother to one of my sons, was clearly my GUARDIAN ANGEL. I love her and miss her dearly.

*Greg Wayton*
*Plain City, Ohio*

# God's Surprising Ways

*This is the story of a successful ministry that thrives and inspires others as it combines faith and exercise.*

Mary, Mother of Jesus, and "kettlebells" are not typically topics that are discussed in the same sentence, but God often reaches us in surprising ways with everyday miracles.

A kettlebell is a ball of iron with a handle. It is a weight-training tool used in various ways that are interesting to both the brain and the body. I'm a strength coach who specializes in teaching adults how to use kettlebells and bodyweight movements safely and efficiently to get stronger, build cardiovascular endurance, and become more mobile and flexible.

One morning I was training in the gym after teaching my early morning strength classes to adults. This day however, as I was swinging a heavy kettlebell, the Hail Mary prayer kept playing over and over in my head and heart like a song stuck on repeat. Something as peaceful as the Hail Mary prayer doesn't really pair well with the heart-pumping intensity of kettlebell swings, so I put the kettlebell down and stood there, hands on my hips, looking at myself curiously in the mirror.

At that time, I offered my kettlebell strength training program out of a dance studio that had mirrors everywhere. When I trained alone, I used the mirrors to keep an eye on my technique. At that moment, with the kettlebell on the ground, and still gazing in the mirror, I realized that something important was happening —Jesus and Mary are having an intervention with me. "Hail Mary, full of grace…" kept rising up in my heart ... what am I doing spending so much time at the gym when there is so much Jesus is calling me to do? Why am I not praying the Rosary anymore?

    I had already been at the gym most of the morning, probably too long. My thoughts turned to my prayer life — I prayed after I finished training most days, but it was often rushed and my prayers didn't feel as heart-felt as they had been before I opened my gym. I realized that I exercised much more than I prayed, and that 'coach' had become a big part of my identity. I was an active in my faith, but I knew deep down that Jesus was asking more of me; I hadn't taken the time to try to figure it out.

    That day however, something shifted in me. I felt the urge to combine prayer and exercise in a way I never had before, even though I knew pairing prayer with heavy kettlebell swings wasn't the answer. I left the gym and returned home, intending to pray the Rosary, and then working on a program to pair prayer and exercise. I also searched the Internet to see if someone had already created an authentically Catholic way to pair prayer and exercise. I looked specifically for Rosary prayers with exercise because I had a strong devotion to Mary and to the Rosary, even though, at that time, I had stopped praying a daily Rosary.

    My Internet search turned up "SoulCore" Rosary prayer with exercise. SoulCore is an invitation to unite the body and soul in prayer, to glorify God to the fullest, and to honor the great gift He has given us by joining our prayers with strength, stretching and functional movement.

    I immediately began the process of applying for the next available SoulCore Discovery Retreat. That event conflicted with a kettlebell coaching event I was expected to attend in Minneapolis, but I declined the kettlebell event, feeling Mary's nudge once more, and feeling confident that this was more important. I was on the SoulCore waiting list, but was admitted at the last minute. Thus I began a new and exciting phase of my spiritual and physical fitness journey.

I became a certified SoulCore leader and began offering SoulCore in parishes around the Columbus diocese. This has been such a blessing as I've met so many faith-filled women who love praying the Rosary and sharing our faith and my love for Mother Mary.

I made another change by closing my gym and moving my strength classes to a local health club so I would have more time to serve Jesus. I have been blessed to do things like attending daily Mass, writing a column for the Catholic Times, recording "Holy and Healthy minutes" for St. Gabriel Catholic Radio, joining a daytime bible study, and attending Adoration.

Mother Mary interceded with me on behalf of her Son and shifted my priorities so that I could live a life truly centered on what matters — knowing, loving, and serving God. I am so thankful! This miracle changed the course of my life and continues to impact me in surprising ways on this amazing journey with Jesus through Mary.

*Lori Crock*

*Dublin, Ohio*

# Our Christmas Angel

*This is an account of my sister's firm belief in "signs" from heaven.*

For some years, my sister Marge has shared her firm belief that our departed loved ones periodically send us "signs" from heaven to let us know that they are still with us, sharing in our everyday experiences and helping us endure life's most difficult challenges. It is perhaps fitting that Marge's home would provide the setting for what occurred on Christmas Eve this past year.

For nearly 30 years, my wife and I and our two daughters faithfully travelled to our hometown of Buffalo, New York to spend Christmas Eve with our families. On many of those occasions, we encountered brutal weather, but we always managed it to make it safely to "Nana Rita's" (my wife's mother) where she warmly greeted us, regardless of the hour, with something to eat and a cool glass of wine or a cold Canadian beer. Our annual retreats to Buffalo at Christmas ended when Nana Rita moved to Florida a few years ago for health reasons. Our extended holiday visits with family in cold snowy Buffalo were replaced with enjoying a few days of warm Florida sunshine with Nana. Then, our Florida trips at Christmas abruptly ended after we said our final goodbyes to our beloved Nana in October of 2012. Thankfully, less than 2 months later, my wife and I greeted our first grandchild whose timely arrival truly helped us endure our heartfelt loss.

Our plans for Christmas 2013 included a return trip to Buffalo, in large part so that our Buffalo family could meet our beautiful granddaughter. Several weeks before Christmas however, our family learned of the inexplicable passing of the son of one of our dearest friends in Columbus. Our Christmas plans were placed on hold as we steadfastly attempted to provide comfort and support to our friends and their family while struggling to understand why God had chosen this warm, loving and talented young man as he was about to graduate from college. My wife and I were devastated by this young man's death and we pledged to his family that we would pray for them and continue to provide support as they learned to live with his loss. At his funeral, my wife calmly but confidently told his mom and dad that our Nana Rita would be sure to look after him in heaven.

My wife and I arrived safely in Buffalo on the evening preceding Christmas Eve. In typical fashion, my sister Marge and my brother-in- law Jim enthusiastically greeted us and soon Marge was serving us warm homemade pot pie and refreshing drinks. As we chatted with our hosts late into the evening (now Christmas Eve) we shared the tragic news of the recent passing of the son of our close friends. Before long, our conversation began to drag as each of us began to internalize and ponder the depth of this family's despair. We all agreed that prayer would help them persevere. With that, I was reminded of my wife's special message to our friends that our own dear Nana Rita would surely be of assistance to their son in heaven.

Suddenly, Marge sprung to her feet to slice another piece of pie and pour another glass of wine and the conversation quickly shifted. The mood in the room lifted as my wife began to speak about how much her mom enjoyed the Christmas season and spending time with family and loved ones. We laughed aloud as we exchanged warm memories of her, including the antlers, dangling ornament earrings and Rudolph nose she enjoyed wearing to our holiday gatherings. She was loved by all. What a gal!

As Marge was about to pour my wife a glass of wine, my wife stopped her, exclaiming, "Look at the ice in my glass!" As we examined her glass, we quickly found that the 3 ice cubes that Marge had randomly tossed into the glass had perfectly formed the body of a beautiful Angel with broad wings and a curved body. Silently, we stared at the glass in total amazement before finally taking a photograph. Seconds after the photograph was taken, the ice cubes collapsed! Instinctively, our eyes moved from the glass to Marge. Intuitively, we knew exactly what she was thinking. "Surely, this was a "sign!"

*(This article was published in* The Catholc Times *in January, 2014.)*

*Dennis J. Morrison*

*Hilliard, Ohio*

# The Relic

*This is the true story of a second-class relic I now carry with me when visiting the sick.*

About fifteen years ago, while showering, I felt a hard lump in my chest. Knowing that men can have breast cancer, I was concerned. After it persisted for a few weeks, I finally saw my Family Practice doctor about it. He examined me and was also concerned, even mentioning that "we might want to biopsy." I put him off, and said I would monitor it closely for a while.

About that same time, I visited my former pastor who was Director of the Jubilee Museum in downtown Columbus. After telling him of my concern about the lump, and asking for his prayers, he retrieved the white zucchetto (skullcap) of Pope John Paul (now Saint John Paul) which the papal nuncio (Cardinal Vigano) had gifted to the museum on his visit there. My former pastor cut a small thread from the cap and carefully glued it to a piece of blue paper. He touched it to my chest while praying over me, gave me the relic, and advised me to get a reliquary (a small gold container for relics) to preserve it and carry it. He also gave me a certificate of authenticity for the relic.

Several weeks later, on my follow-up visit to my doctor, the lump had completely disappeared! The doctor was completely surprised and called it "a miracle." I thank the Lord every time I carry it, and have used it many times to bless the people I visit who are homebound or in hospitals and nursing homes.

*Deacon Anthony C. Bonacci*
*Plain City, Ohio*

# God Provides

*This is the story of a dedicated parishioner, the "miracle" of her obtaining funding for a parish outreach center, and the continued miracles of supplying that center.*

In the spring of 2008, a few months after my parish opened its beautiful new Parish Activity Center, a casual conversation with my pastor sparked an idea that became my daily focus for the following year. I remarked to him that I wished the building had another wing which could house our Outreach Mission Center. It had become difficult to store furniture and household items collected for poor and needy families.

Our "St. Martin's Outreach Group" had been formed in the mid 90's with 8-10 active members. We accepted donations of furniture and household items and stored them in our basements, garages and barns until we learned of someone in need. We even delivered them to their home. It was a very rewarding ministry.

My pastor suggested I submit a Grant proposal to the Diocesan Catholic Foundation. Never having written a Grant proposal before, I jotted down tips and read about the process online. A category under "Evangelization and Help for Poor and Needy" seemed to fit. I finished my Grant proposal and submitted it just under the deadline. My pastor was out of the country at the time and didn't have an opportunity to review it. I held my breath and prayed. A few weeks later, I learned that we did NOT get the Grant. I was disappointed but determined.

In January of the following year, my pastor told me another Grant cycle had been announced. I was ready! He reviewed my first proposal and suggested valuable pointers and tips to make it more appealing to the Foundation's Grant Committee. With the help of several others, I added graphs and some demographic information, and demonstrated how we were networking to find leads and identify the needs in our area.

The second proposal was selected, and we were awarded $25,000 to construct our storage center! Not wasting any time, we solicited three bids from contractors to construct the building and selected a small Amish company with whom we felt comfortable. We held a ground breaking after Mass the following Sunday and the site preparation by Parish members began the next day. The following week, the material arrived along with the Amish crew. It took them only 3 1/2 days to erect the building! A few days later, we were officially up and running!

One month later, we asked our Bishop to attend and bless our building and the undertaking of the work we were doing. It was a wonderful day and a very proud moment when the Bishop told us how deeply grateful he was for this undertaking and how he wished every parish in the Diocese would do something similar.

Soon, we had social workers contacting us on their clients' behalf. We developed a system and organized everything so we could run the Center like a small business. We filled every request we received if we had the items on hand to give. We soon learned what the most frequent needs were and tried to always have those things in inventory. Some items were very difficult to have on hand so we just could not fill the request. Washers and dryers and other major appliances were always in short supply. Still, miracles do happen!

Some cases stood out when we simply could not fill the need. WE couldn't but God could! We would pray and hope for gift donations of things we needed, and suddenly those items would appear. It has happened too many times to be a coincidence!

## *Examples*:

- A lift chair for a handicapped man suddenly appeared the day before his brother was picking up a truckload of items.

- On one occasion, we tried to give a family twin beds but they would not fit their tiny bedroom. But the morning we were making a delivery, a parishioner called and offered a nice set of bunk beds.

- A donated humidifier for twin babies with lung issues and twin car seats for them when they seriously outgrew their existing seats.

- My husband was driving home from a donation pick up and the wind blew a bed destined for a family off the truck. A man stopped to help him, and as they were carrying the debris off the highway, he told my husband to follow him to his home. He had a like-new bed he would donate.

- After praying for a religious icon for the flower bed by our building, a parishioner called and offered a small statue of Mother Mary with a baby Jesus in her arms. Later, another talented member of our parish restored and repainted the statue for all to enjoy.

The examples of little miracles continue to this day, encouraging us to believe and encouraging us to pray for what is needed. For 15 years we have thanked God for our many blessings and for our mission center where we help restore hope to families in need. We try never to take anything for granted. This is God's world and we exist at his pleasure. May we continue to be worthy of HIS BLESSINGS.

*Gloria Butler*

*Plain City, Ohio*

# In the Blink of an Eye... There was Hope

*This is the inspiring story of a horse lover who to this day never gives up hope.*

I feel compelled to share a story that has been etched in my brain for over 20 years. My life has not turned out as I expected, but I have found peace. Recently, sitting in church, I felt God urging me to share this story to help someone else.

It was a bone chilling, windy and rainy December day in Central Ohio. The parking lot of the riding stable was crowded, and children's voices could be heard from the driveway entrance. The grounds were immaculately kept and the barn paneling was more beautiful than one would see in a home.

My sisters and I had boarded our horses at this stable for years and knew everyone. On this particular day I brought my younger cousin Ivana, who was not familiar with horses but who wanted see my horse "Traveler." The enormous indoor arena was filled with children, parents looking on, and horse lessons in full swing.

Ivana was riding Traveler and I was walking beside them when my attention was suddenly drawn to the adjacent barn. It took a minute for me to comprehend what I was seeing - smoke billowing from the far end of the barn. I could hear Terry, the trainer yelling for help and needing water. I rushed to the wash stall, grabbed the hose, turned on the water and ran the hose to the now smoke filled utility room.

The water came out in a small stream. "I need pressure, get me pressure!" yelled Terry. Quickly, I scanned the long hose for kinks as the smoke began to infiltrate the aisle. My heart was racing and my mind rushing, unsure what to do next. I hesitantly chose to run into the barn office, snatch up the phone, and call 911. I was shaking, every word burning in my throat as I tried to relay the urgency to the operator, who calmly kept asking me to repeat the information. Frustrated, I yelled, "There are children and horses in here; WE NEED HELP NOW!" It became difficult to breathe, my eyes were burning, and the office was now filled with smoke. I gave one last attempt to convey the information and had to get out. As I ran down the aisle, I opened all the stall doors, hoping to give the horses a chance of survival.

    Close to the exit door was a young panicked saddle bred tied outside a stall pulling and lunging, trying to break loose. I freed the yearling and ran him into the arena which now seemed to be muffled chaos. People were crying and screaming and the horses were frantic. I handed off the stressed yearling and ran back into the barn only to be pushed back by the intense heat and smoke. In a blink of an eye the huge barn filled with thick smoke, and I knew there was no going back in.

    My attention turned to finding my horse and Ivana. In the distance I saw Traveler barreling against the pasture gate desperately trying to join the herd. Ivana was hopelessly trying to control him from the ground. The rain and wind had now picked up and stung on contact. The air was black with cinders and the grass began to catch fire. Frantic people began running to the far end of the pasture to safety. The gate was damaged, and we couldn't force it open. The only option was to get Traveler into the small empty barn that opened into the neighboring pasture. Running toward the far exit door, my heart sank as I saw what appeared to be bundles of twine and baling wire securing the large sliding door tightly shut. Tears filled my eyes as we desperately tried to untangle the mess. Traveler was running back and forth in the aisle, his saddle half off, and his bridle in pieces. We could hear the crackling flames against the entrance door. "Where was the fire department?" I thought. "Time is running out!"

For the first time that day I had no plan and no hope. With frozen fingers we continued to frantically work to loosen the door barrier but knew in our hearts it was impossible. Then out of nowhere came a nondescript man I did not recognize. From his pocket he pulled out a pocket knife and without a word sliced through the aged wire and twine like it was butter. Quickly I removed the remaining gear from Traveler and the dark barn lit up as the door slid open. Traveler galloped to join the other horses.

Ivana and I ran through the thick mud toward the safety of the pasture. We stood in awe and extreme sadness as the fire department watered down the perimeter of the barn having no choice but to let it burn to the ground. The three alarm fire took the lives of fourteen horses and the three legged office dog that courageously would not leave his post.

Later that day I learned that the trainer safely got out and saved many horses which he had released into the front yard. Despite my relentless effort to find and thank the man who saved us, no one knew who he was. The stable owner, a kind gentle man who loved nature and animals, had few words that day except to inquire about the 911 call. I told him I had made the call. With a puzzled look he quietly said "I don't know how you got through... the phone lines have been down all day!" I now know without a doubt that nondescript man was an angel. I also know that as tragic as that day was, several miracles occurred.

Today, as I struggle with a rare debilitating muscle disorder, making it difficult to even walk, I can only dream of riding a horse again. It would be much easier to just give up. However, I believe God gave me that dismal December day to help me now during these challenging times, to find the good amongst the bad, to know miracles do happen, and to never give up hope.

*Sandra Hilbert*

*Plain City, Ohio*

# Waiting For Her Guardian Angel

*This is the true story of my mother-in-law's guardian angel.*

Most Western New Yorkers vividly remember "The Blizzard of 1977", when near zero temperatures, wind gusts peaking at more than 70 m.p.h., and three feet of freshly fallen snow combined to create what some have called "the storm of the century." Many also remember the ice storm that besieged the same area the previous spring.

Cold rainy weather during the month of March is the norm in my hometown of Buffalo, New York. On this evening however, the all-day rain had turned to sleet and before long, the city was blanketed in ice. Roads became too treacherous to travel and most businesses (large and small) closed early. Not surprisingly, power outages became widespread as mature trees succumbed to the weight of the ice on their branches resulting in downed power lines. Local officials instructed residents to remain indoors if possible.

Like many storms, this one arrived without warning. Many people were simply stranded, and others were challenged with the prospect of a slow, dangerous ride home. In the latter category was my future mother-in-law Rita. On that evening, Rita was at a friend's house with her card group playing bridge. The group had not been aware of the weather conditions outside until Rita's daughter (my girlfriend Mary at the time) phoned to alert them. Accustomed to stormy weather (having lived her entire life in Buffalo), Rita rose to the challenge and began the short drive home. She would explain later her perception that she was the only motorist on the road. There were no signs of life, and the only sounds were those of falling tree limbs and her windshield wipers attempting to clear the heavy sleet, which had continued to fall.

Her journey home nearly complete, Rita found her street impassable. As she parked her car at the corner of her street, a stranger suddenly approached her and explained to her that there were tree limbs and power lines littering her street and sidewalks and that he would need to accompany her home. Gently taking her by the arm and using his flashlight as a beacon to guide their footsteps, he slowly and safely guided Rita to her front door. However, he vanished into the night as quickly as he had appeared!

The next day, Rita learned that her neighbor had returned home the previous evening, literally minutes after Rita, but that the "helpful stranger" had not been there to assist her. Oddly, while word of the stranger's kindness spread throughout Rita's close-knit community, no one had seen him that night nor was anyone ever able to identify him. Of her encounter with the stranger, she would say, "He was my Guardian Angel whose job that evening was to see to it that I arrived home safely." How could we argue with her explanation?

Nearly 35 years after her mysterious encounter with the stranger, and at a very healthy age of 96, Rita suffered a massive stroke while living in her retirement center in Lakewood Ranch, Florida. The stroke was devastating, leaving her partially paralyzed and unable to speak. We were devastated, as Rita had always been the "rock" around which our large extended family had revolved. In the difficult days that followed, my wife and other devoted family members took turns keeping vigil at Rita's bedside. Several weeks later, at a time when our family was finally prepared to let her go, Rita passed on. As we grieved, we took solace in our belief that on the morning of her passing, Rita's "Guardian Angel" once again arrived in her time of need to take her safely "home" once more ...

*Dennis J. Morrison*

*Hilliard, Ohio*

   *(This article was published in The Catholic Times Nov. 2012)*

# Mass at Camp

*This is the story of a devout Scout leader and his experience of God's presence in a very special way.*

My upbringing was like most others who went through twelve years of Catholic schools and were part of a practicing Catholic family. After I had grown, married, and had children of my own, I started feeling a need to more than just attend Mass. My thoughts were that this had been a mere obligation. I attended Mass faithfully, but mostly because I knew it was expected of all Catholics – it was even elevated to the status of a 'Commandment of the Church'.

In response, I started to set aside time for prayer, a regular period for reading scripture, and looked for some way to more actively participate in the Mass itself. I also longed to get into scouting and pondered going into the inner city to work with kids who had less opportunity to join such a program. When I shared this with a neighbor, he asked me if I would consider starting a troop in my own church, as theirs had folded a few years earlier. I was hooked! This was the start of my tenure as a scoutmaster in my own parish.

This was a Catholic troop and we participated in all the Catholic aspects of scouting, including Scout Sunday, the "Ad Altari Dei" award, a "Day of Recollection" campout, going into town in uniform for Mass on camping weekends, and even having Mass at the camp for larger gatherings, such as district-wide or area-wide events.

At one of these district camps, we had Mass in the administration building with a Jesuit priest from an area high school and all the Catholic scouts from area troops in attendance. From the time of the Gospel reading and through the consecration, I had become very emotional, feeling that I sensed the presence of Christ Himself. After receiving Communion, I returned to my seat at the back and I was suddenly overcome with a wondrous sense of awe – I sensed the brightest white light, all around me, and I saw nothing else. I just sat there, weeping and trembling. Absolutely no doubt that God was making His presence known.

I let my assistant scoutmaster know that I needed to be by myself and he said to go ahead. I left the building, knowing only that God was present as I had never known Him before. I was gone by myself for what I later learned was about two hours. The whole time I was reeling in awe trying to fathom what and why this was happening. I had no sense of anything else happening, nor my going anywhere or watching anything. I was caught up in the splendor of His presence. God chose this way to let me know He is real and is with us in the Mass and the Eucharist, the view I hold to this day.

After about two hours, my mind came back to near normal and I realized where I was, so I headed the half mile back to our camp site, wondering the whole time about how I would lead the boys in wrapping up.

When I got back, I found everything packed up, apparently spearheaded by my assistant and the senior patrol leader. Even my tent and personal gear were packed and ready to go. Nothing was said by me or to me about this experience, but I believe my assistant had a pretty good idea.

Communion time at Mass was, for quite a while, almost a reliving of the incident, but as time went on, the intensity and the frequency subsided. Every now and then, I get the feeling during Mass similar to that day and rejoice in knowing He is here and that He loves me.

*Joe Humphrey*

*Plain City, Ohio*

# September 12-
# A God-Incident?

*Perhaps this "co-incident" was God's re-assurance that we were meant to be together.*

My wife Elaine had been my "steady" through five years of college. We typically dated on Saturday night, when her father Herman would be sitting on the front porch, even in the winter, watching through the window Jackie Gleason's "The Honeymooners" show on TV. Herman was a WW I veteran and had served in the Gas Corps.; as a result, he had serious breathing problems and emphysema. He always called me "kid." I'm sorry he didn't live to see us married or to enjoy his grandchildren.

When Herman passed on February 12, 1964, my Mom and Dad respectfully attended the wake because they had known him as the neighborhood plumber, and because "Tony has been dating this girl for a few years now." When Mom sat next to Elaine's mother Margaret at the visitation, she expressed her sympathy and asked, "Margaret, what year were you and Herman married?" Margaret replied, "1942." Mom said, "Hmm, Carmen and I were married that year." She then asked what month. Margaret replied, "September," Mom said, "Hmm, Carmen and I were married in September." She then asked what date in September. Margaret replied, "September 12." Mom exclaimed, "My goodness, Margaret, we were married on the same day!" So Elaine's folks and mine were married on the same day in the same year, in the same city!

"September 12" was very special to us all our married life, and as it turned out, we moved into our home in Plain City seven years later, on September 12!

*Deacon Anthony C. Bonacci*

*Plain City, Ohio*

# My Daughter Survived

*This is the story of a guardian angel protecting a young lady at the scene of a terrible accident.*

It was dusk as my daughter Laura was travelling home from work. She was just a few miles from home on the state highway when the right side of her van went off the road. Travelling at the speed limit of 55 mph, she overcompensated trying to get back on the road. She veered off the right side of the road, through a ditch, and rolled the van end to end until the vehicle ended in a field up about 30 feet from the road. Her van was now facing in the opposite direction she was originally heading and was resting on the driver's side. A woman who was driving in the opposite direction saw what had happened, stopped, and called 911 right away.

A man across the field on his motorcycle heard the van go off the road and drove over to see how he could help. This is his description of what he saw: "When I got there, the van was on its side. No windows were broken, but the van was badly damaged. I was about to break through the windshield when I saw her standing up on what would be the driver's side door, so I climbed up on the top (the passenger side) and was able to open the passenger door to help her out. As I was about to ease her down the windshield to the ground, a young man appeared, took her ankles, and helped to guide her safely to the ground. It was about that time that I heard the sirens from the emergency vehicles approaching. The young man said 'I have to go' and he left. I never saw where he came from or where he went. He just kind of showed up, and then he wasn't there."

The phone rang. My daughter, Laura, sounded shaken on the other end. She said, "Dad, I'm okay, but I wrecked the van." I rushed to the site of the accident to get Laura. She was being attended to by an EMT and had sustained a bruise on her left hip, but had no other injuries. I inspected the van and discovered no windows were broken and the air bag had not deployed. Inside, the van was a mess. It had passed in between two power poles on the side of the road and debris was scattered all over the ground. The woman who saw the accident and called 911 said that she saw the van "upside down about 10 feet in the air." There was no reason to think that anyone in that vehicle had not been badly injured or killed.

Sometime later as I spoke with Laura about that evening, she said it suddenly came to her: "It was dusk and kind of dark when I went off the road. And I remember that when that young man grabbed my ankles to help me down, it was like the middle of the day! Everything was so bright! I can't explain what it was like!" She cried as she recounted what she had experienced.

Miracle? No doubt. Guardian Angel? I'm convinced. Each year on October 2 (the Memorial of the Holy Guardian Angels), I am brought to tears and pray in thanksgiving for the gift of my daughter Laura. I text her each year on that day and remind her of the love of God, and how each of us have our own Guardian Angel to watch over us.

*Deacon Doug Mould*
*Coshocton, Ohio*

# Grandpa's Baby Patrick

*This is the story of a family receiving the gift of new life at the same time they were saying "farewell" to their loved one.*

On Wednesday, April 22, 2020, I went to my father's home to give him a haircut and help him get ready for his late morning doctor's visit. It was probably 9:45AM when I arrived to find the lights off and received no reply when I called his name. I walked quietly to his bedroom to wake him and found him still in his pajamas under the covers.

When I gently touched his hand, I realized that my Dad had died in his sleep. He looked peaceful and warm in his bed, although he was cool to the touch. I immediately called his doctor to report the situation and ask what I should do next. After hanging up with my father's doctor, I called my two sisters to tell them the news and ask them to come to our father's home.

When my youngest sister arrived, she shared the news that her third grandchild had been born at 10:54PM on Tuesday, April 21, 2020. We believe that when our Lord decided it was time for His angels to bring home faithful servant Frank Everson, He also decided it was time for His angels to help my great nephew Patrick James Greger to be born.

Our family finds great comfort in visualizing Frank on the upward path to ***heaven*** (led by angels and my Mom, Betty) while baby Patrick was being led to ***earth*** by other angels and his Great Grandma Betty. Although my father was pronounced dead on April 22nd, we were never given an exact time of death and we believe he may have died at the same moment baby Patrick was born.  Our guardian angels are just one of so many blessings from God.

*Angela Everson Ray*

*Columbus, Ohio*

# My Conversion

*This is the story of a young lady's search for the true faith and her witness to the Real Presence.*

I am a convert to the Catholic faith. I was raised as a Missouri Synod Lutheran, and although its services were similar to Mass, I always believed that Holy Communion was the true body and blood of Christ.

During our engagement, my future husband and I spoke frequently to a local Catholic priest who was a knowledgeable apologist. On one occasion he questioned me, "If Lutherans believe in the true presence of Christ, what do they do with the 'leftovers?'"

At that time, I was going to Catholic Mass on Saturdays and to a local Lutheran church service on Sundays, trying to discern where my church home should be. On the very next Sunday after being questioned by the priest, I was walking through the parking lot following the Lutheran service. Suddenly, the sacristy door opened, and a man casually threw the contents of the communion cup onto the gravel parking lot. To me, it felt like a slap in the face – I was truly meant to see this!

The priest's question had been answered. As the bible says, (Matt.:28.20) "...And behold, I am with you always, until the end of the age." And in John 6:51, Jesus says, "I am the living bread which has come down from heaven. Anyone who eats this bread will live forever; and the bread that I shall give is my flesh, for the life of the world."

I thought, "Shouldn't we always err on the side of caution when the Lord is clear on his teaching about the Eucharist? Jesus told us clearly He is truly present to us in the Eucharist and says He is with us always." At that moment I knew I had found my church home!

That same local priest became a valued friend who prepared us for Matrimony and presided for our marriage on October 12, 1996. The following Spring at the Easter Vigil service, he administered the sacrament of Confirmation, receiving me fully into the Catholic faith. From that time on, my husband and I have been active members of that same Catholic parish.

*Jennifer Donovan*

*Plain City, Ohio*

# A Sudden Passing

*This is the story of the sudden loss of a spouse, and the little miracles that his family was blessed with after his passing.*

On April 22, 2022, I received a call from my youngest son while I was at work. He said he was in the area and wanted to stop by my office. I thought that was a bit unusual but hoped that perhaps he was interested in seeing where I worked and what I did at work. Sadly, when he arrived, he hugged me and said, "Mom, this is the hardest thing I've ever had to do." He told me that his Dad, my husband, had died that day in a motorcycle accident. (I later learned that his passing was very quick and that he did not suffer for long.) My husband had mentioned more than once that he wanted to pass quickly like his Mom. She had been cooking in her kitchen, had a stroke, and died shortly thereafter. I thought, "Thank You, Lord" for answering his prayer.

On so many days, the reality of this incident is so difficult to believe. Our almost 40 years of marriage together and my routine of sharing life with someone was suddenly gone. We didn't have a perfect marriage, but I don't think anyone does. There were some very unhappy times and some very good times.

We had married when I was five and a half months pregnant. At that time, my mom was very angry with me, as any Christian mother would be, but that's how we started married life together. We were determined to make it work even though the circumstances were less than ideal.

As a faith-filled person, I started looking for positives after my husband's death. There were several I discovered:

First, my husband was on that ill-fated motorcycle trip with his brother and another friend. I am now so grateful that my husband was with his brother when it happened, as his brother has a very strong personality and was there to comfort my husband at the end. He handled everything with *grace*. (I would not have handled the situation very well at all.)

Second, I wanted to have our previous pastor, (who had been my boss for 9 years), to celebrate the funeral Mass. He had spent time with our family while our pastor, had golfed with my husband, and was instrumental in our children's faith formation. In deference to our current pastor, I called to ask him if our previous pastor could concelebrate the funeral Mass. He was very gracious, and apologized that he wouldn't be available due to a prior commitment, so we were able to have our former pastor celebrate the Mass.

Third, the week after my husband passed, my youngest son, who had informed me of my husband's passing, called me one night to say that he "needed to come back to church" and would be coming back to Mass with me. He has kept his word. Even if I am away on Sunday, he attends Mass on his own. I consider this to be a miracle... a real blessing, as my children had left the Catholic faith as adults, and this had been a huge sadness for me.

My son had struggled as a teen and my husband and I had worried about him and his future. I had been praying to the Blessed Mother for several years for them to find their way back to the faith. Our Blessed Mother Mary had come through for my son, and I have faith and trust that the other two children may return, while I continue to trust Mary and God's timing.

Fourth, our daughter and son-in-law had divorced after 7 years of marriage. They have a daughter together and to their credit, they work graciously in sharing their time with her and dealing with other parent details. My daughter's ex-husband visited the week of my husband's funeral and spent time at our house. He was very comfortable with everyone in the family despite the divorce. I was so grateful that he and our daughter spent their time together so kindly that week.

Fifth, about eleven years ago, our son and his wife had a dog that had several puppies. My husband really wanted one of the pups, but not being a pet person, this was a real sacrifice for me. I complained more than I should have about having a pet, but my husband was in love with our pup "Lodi." Just before he left for the motorcycle trip, he noticed that Lodi's back legs weren't working correctly. He took her to the vet who put her on steroids, but said she had a condition that wasn't going to get better. My husband was not an emotional person, but I could tell this news really upset him. I told him to go on his trip and not worry about it, and that we would deal with it after he got home. Fortunately, he didn't have to be there when my sons had to have Lodi euthanized. We later scattered some of her ashes on my husband's grave. It seemed appropriate.

Finally, the most astounding miracle of all occurred a few weeks before my husband died. As I stated earlier, he was not an emotional man, but he and I were sitting in his wood shop one evening enjoying a drink and talking. Out of the blue he said something like, *"If something happens to me tomorrow, I've had a great life, good and kind kids, and wonderful grandkids. I've gotten to do so many things I've wanted to do."* Could this comment from my husband have been a greater miracle for me and my children? He and God were letting me know that all would be ok. And it is!

After several months of thinking about the passing of my husband and its aftermath, I've concluded that there are many miracles to be found if we keep our faith-eyes open. Even in tragedy miracles can be found.

*Anonymous*

# My Guardian Angel in the Snow

*This is a story about a young woman's protection by her guardian angel.*

When I was a little girl, my grandmother taught me about guardian angels. For me, the concept is as difficult to understand now as it was then. That is, until a cold, snowy February morning in Columbus, Ohio in 1982.

My husband Joe and I were married in October of 1981 and assumed a mortgage on a small ranch on the west side of Columbus. Joe had recently graduated and took a job on the East side of Columbus while I was working at Huntington Bank on the North side.

We each left for work at 7:15 a.m. and made our way to the freeway. We drove the same route for the first half of our commute, one following the other. Once we reached downtown, I would take the ramp onto I-71 North and Joe would continue on I-70 East. At the split, we would drive side-by-side and wave goodbye to each other.

On this February morning, we woke up to snow. Driving was a bit tricky. The snowplows had been working that morning, pushing most of the snow out of the driving lanes and onto the berm of the freeway. As I followed my husband, I became concerned about the salt spray from Joe's car building up on my windshield and impairing my view. I remember pushing my windshield washer button several times to improve my view.

At the downtown split, we waved as usual. As I entered the Northbound ramp onto I-71, my focus intensified as I was now dealing with blowing snow and fast-moving traffic. I moved into the right-hand lane where I felt more comfortable at a slower speed.

My car apparently hit an icy patch, but it happened so quickly I couldn't react by steering, braking, or avoiding a dangerous spin. I was terrified as my car settled to a stop in the left-hand lane facing the center median. I was perpendicular to the berm, with traffic approaching my driver's door. Frozen by fear, I focused on the headlights of a very large city bus approaching my driver's door. That's when my guardian angel stepped in.

At the back of my car, a strange man was pushing my car into the median. Fortunately, he was able to push my small car out of the path of the bus. He then pounded on my back window and yelled "Drive!" Without thinking, I pushed in the clutch, found first gear, and moved forward and out of traffic.

After a very short distance, I stopped and rolled down my window and yelled "Thank You!" only to find no one was there. Looking around, I realized no one was walking away from my car; no one was in front or behind me; no other car had pulled over. Then it struck me that this man must be my guardian angel!

Throughout most of my young life, I had been an active Catholic, leading prayer, and teaching Religious Education classes. I had learned that in times of distress, I could always pray, *"Jesus Save Me."* But as I sat on the freeway on that cold, icy February morning expecting an imminent collision and crushing by a city bus, I was frozen by fear and shear panic. I didn't have time to pray or think about holy intervention.

Now, looking back, I have a new comprehension of guardian angels and how they work. Fortunately for us, guardian angels don't wait for a prayer or even acknowledgment of their existence. We don't need to pray, ask, or beg for their help. They just appear to save us and then return to their invisible state. God has consigned us into their care, and they don't disappoint.

*Karen Martin*

*Hilliard, Ohio*

# Inspired by an Angel

*This is the story of an inspired person intervening and perhaps saving another person's life.*

I like to write! I'm a person who writes handwritten Christmas letters to my friends and family because it brings me joy. When I am composing something important, I often feel inspired, but one time was very different. When I read the Bible, the inspired Word of God, I often wondered, "How does that work? How did the author know what to write?"

In 2001, my family was part of a cancer support group. In our weekly sharing, we supported each other in our concerns, anger, suffering & joy. One week, a wife in our group shared that her husband was talking about taking his own life. He had suffered for many years with a terminal diagnosis, but the thought of what suicide would do to their children and his soul was weighing heavily on her.

The next day on my way to work, I couldn't shake the feeling that I was meant to intervene. I remember like it was yesterday, the words of a letter being spoken into my mind and heart, word for word. Was this an angel inspiring me to write to this man?

I rushed to write the words down when I got to my office and mailed the letter anonymously. The next week when we met, his wife updated us. The letter had changed his course. He began praying the Rosary with another patient in our group, and several months later he passed peacefully, surrounded by his loving family.

*Patty Brown  Mount Sterling, Ohio*

# "Hooking" Brought Me Closer to Him

*This is the story of an artist's spiritual growth through her craft.*

I'm a "hooker." I've always loved fiber arts, and rug hooking is my favorite. I first learned about it over twenty-five years ago when I was intrigued by a magazine article. The projects are made by pulling strips of fabric through a woven base such as linen or rug warp. Like many crafts, it is also an art. Drawing a pattern and color planning make it an artistic endeavor. I've attended workshops and I have developed friendships and relationships that reach well beyond the time spent "hooking." May I tell you about the most impactful one of all...

I've "hooked" everything from small, primitive-looking flowers to detailed pieces measuring three feet by five feet. "Hooking" is so ingrained in my psyche that whenever I see something artistic or colorful, I ponder the possibility of a "hooked" piece. That's where my mind turned when I read about "Smiling Jesus" in Father James Martin's book, *The Jesuit Guide to Almost Everything*. As I'm prone to do in this age of Google, I searched online to find images of Jesus smiling. There were many. I wondered, "How come I'd never seen Jesus like this?"

As much as I wanted to do a "hooked" piece of Jesus smiling, I was hesitant because I knew it would be difficult to "hook" a realistic face, and it would be even harder to "hook"

Jesus. I had to do it right; after all, Jesus would be watching!

One interesting thing that happened as I chose the wool for Jesus' face was that I realized He wasn't Caucasian! He was a dark-skinned, dark-haired Jew. He was a real person with human looks and traits. I had never really "looked" at Jesus or thought about his human features. He was the guy in robes, his arms raised to the sky as he spoke to crowds of people.

I thought, "Wait a minute. He didn't just preach to crowds of people; He spent time with his 12 best buddies — fishing, eating, and laughing." I had never thought of Him that way before.

I got down to business on the project. My "hooked" Jesus had to have smiling eyes and a grin. I "hooked" his eyes, removed them, and hooked them again. And Jesus smiled at me as I did it. Some days He flat-out laughed. Sometimes I looked at what I'd "hooked" the day before and knew I had to redo it.

"Hooking" reflects life. We have good days when everything goes just right; we have bad days when nothing works. And all the while Jesus watches. As I "hooked" His face, He became a friend, and I developed a different relationship with Him. *I felt like He was physically present.*

He'd always been there with me; I just wasn't conscious of it. I had only talked to Jesus in church or when I needed His help with something. Now, I share my laughs. Now, I'm aware of His presence when I don't know what to do about some problem in my life, and I feel Him say, *"It will be okay. I'm here."* Now, I feel His presence as He looks over at me from the "hooked" piece that hangs on the wall in our family room.

"Hooking" brought me closer to Jesus. Who would have thought it?

*Jan Grose*

*Plain City, Ohio*

# About The Author

Deacon Anthony C. Bonacci is Assistant Dean Emeritus, College of Pharmacy, The Ohio State University. He is the father of four adult children, Lynn Marie (Chapman), Tina Marie (Hardin), Maria Margaret (Lentz), and Anthony G. Bonacci. Deacon Bonacci has been a member of Saint Joseph the Worker parish, Plain City, Ohio, for 52 years, and an ordained deacon for the Diocese of Columbus, Ohio, for 26 years.

He was married to his wife Elaine for 53 years until her untimely passing in 2019. Deacon Bonacci has eight grandchildren ranging in age from 31 years of age to seven years of age. He has published articles in *Marriage Encounter* magazine, *Deacon Digest* magazine, *The Catholic Times* of Columbus, *The American Journal of Hospital Pharmacy*, *Tetrahedron Letters*, and local newsletters of the *Marriage Encounter* and *Cursillo* movements. This is Deacon Bonacci's third book.

www.ingramcontent.com/pod-product-compliance
Lightning Source LLC
Chambersburg PA
CBHW070654050426
42451CB00008B/351